A NURSE'S TOUCH

A prayer and devotional guide for nurses. Volume 1

TOMEKIA Y. LUCKETT, PHD, RN

A Nurse's Touch: A prayer and devotional guide for nurses

Volume 1

By Tomekia Y. Luckett, PhD, RN

© 2018, Dr. Tomekia Yvette Enterprises LLC

www.drtomekia.com

Email: dr.tomekia@positionedforpurpose.com

Published by Dr.Tomekia Yvette Enterprises LLC

Cover Design by prodesignx

Author photograph by Beth Hemeter

(The Image Maker)

www.imagemakerinc.morephotos.net

I dedicate this book to my forever number one, Thank you Lord, for without you, I am nothing! Truly, with God, all things are possible (Matthew 19:26). Thank you for choosing me for this great purpose. I love you!

To all of my nurse colleagues around the world, this one is for you! May the words of this devotional empower you to fulfill your great calling to serve others!

To my children, my sons, Tamerrious, Tamerrion, and Tamerrick, you three are my greatest joy and inspiration. I love each of you with every fiber of my being.

Contents

Chapter 5

Chapter 6

Chapter 7

Chapter 8

Introduction

Let's get started! Being a nurse is an exciting, and rewarding calling. However, it is also challenging and not an undertaking for the faint of heart. The call as a nurse can present complications, such as emotional, mental and physical stress. As a veteran nurse and nurse educator, I am greatly acquainted with the rewards and challenges of a career in nursing. This short and powerful devotional is designed with you, "the busy nurse" in mind. The design is structured in a head-to-toe systematic manner, to apply Godly principles in our daily work. Inspiring prayers, motivational devotionals, and encouraging scriptures have been created just for you. Allow the word of God to take root in your heart and remind you of the divine call of God in your life to serve as a nurse.

Chapter 1

~THE MIND~

The Mind

Through my many years as a nurse, I remain in awe of the power of the mind. The mind stores our thoughts, memories, emotions, and serves as the control center for our bodily functions. During my tenure as a floor nurse, I worked for a length of time in a geriatric setting. My main patients were those diagnosed with dementia and Alzheimer's. I was always left with a lump in my throat when I observed families visit patients who could not remember their loved ones who so diligently visited them. The patients at times were lost, and afraid as it must be pretty scary to forget who you are, where you are, and why you are there. One of the fascinating findings that has left me amazed all of these years is how these patients who were unable to recall family, friends, and time could still remember God. I would listen intently as they would simply say, "Oh Lord" or sing an old hymn such as "Precious Lord." How is it possible that they could not remember anything else, yet they could always remember God? I have a personal belief. My theory is that there is a place within every one of us where only God can reach. Senility is no match for the power of God! How precious are the ones who entrust their minds to God?

Devotional 1

Think about such things

"Finally, brothers and sisters, whatever is true, whatever is noble, whatever is right, whatever is pure, whatever is lovely, whatever is admirable—if anything is excellent or praiseworthy—think about such things."

Philippians 4:8

Have you ever noticed when you focus on a problem, your body begins to take notice? Feeding your mind with negative thoughts and energy can result in physical symptoms. What are you feeding your mind? There is power in the word of God. The word of God is the greatest weapon against negative thinking. Here is a challenge for you: whenever negative thoughts begin to flood your mind, take the time to replace it with the word of God and positive thinking.

Prayer: Father, in the name of Jesus, help me to think about lovely things each and every day. When I am experiencing an inner battle remind me of the promises presented in Your word. In the mighty name of Jesus, Amen.

Devotional 2

The Transformed Mind

"Do not conform to the pattern of this world, but be transformed by the renewing of your mind. Then you will be able to test and approve what God's will is—his good, pleasing and perfect will."

Romans 12:2

The word transformation can simply be defined as a change. Further, a renewal refers to making something new again. In reading this portion of scripture, it becomes evident that we are to change our mind by making it new. How can we make our mind new? In order to make it new, we would need to change or replace the old. Replace the old way of thinking, negative thoughts and self-doubt. Spending time daily with God in prayer, and studying the word will help you to renew your mind daily.

Prayer: Father, in the name of Jesus, help me each day to renew my mind. Build and strengthen my mind through the word of God. In the mighty name of Jesus, Amen.

Devotional 3

Set your mind above

"Set your minds on things above, not on earthly things."

Colossians 3:2

In our daily work and the overwhelming responsibility of caring for others, we can become frustrated. How do you respond to these challenges? It is important to remember that our career is more than a job, it is a calling. We are called to serve others, and we must serve in our calling as unto the Lord. When you become overwhelmed with call lights, an unending list of tasks, more medications to administer than you can count, remember the calling and your great reward in heaven.

Prayer: Father, in the name of Jesus help me to set my mind on heavenly things. In my calling and when I am tempted, allow me to remember the humility of Christ. In the mighty name of Jesus, Amen.

Chapter 2

~THE EYES~

The Eyes

The ability to see is one of God' most precious gifts. The eyes provide our frame of reference for the world and allow us to see the beauty of creation. We see outwardly, but others cannot see inwardly. The eyes do not allow others to see the inward pain behind the smile or the fear behind the anger. We must learn to see the world through the eyes of Jesus. When confronted by a difficult patient, family, or personal issue take a moment and see the situation through the eyes of Jesus. Jesus, so loving, compassionate, and kind. When our Lord and savior Jesus walked the earth he restored sight to the blind. Can you imagine being blind from birth, or blind for years and then all of a sudden have sight? How splendid and marvelous are the works of the Lord! Lord, help me to see as You see, and love others as according to Your perfect will.

Devotional 4

The lamp of your body

"Your eye is the lamp of your body. When your eyes are healthy, your whole body also is full of light. But when they are unhealthy, your body also is full of darkness."

Luke 11:34

As we work in our calling as servants of Jesus Christ, we will find that our enemies at times may be many. Some people will, in fact, speak harshly and act in an unseemly manner even when we have done nothing to deserve it. Have you ever worked with a difficult patient or family? I can remember an occasion with a patient where whatever I did, it seemed not to be enough. It is easy to become frustrated and act out of character in this type of situation. However, we must remember to fix our eyes on Christ. Your eyes illuminate the body, and you must strive to keep your eyes full of the light of Christ.

Prayer: Father, in the name of Jesus, let me see the world through the eyes of Jesus Christ. Help me to firmly fix my eyes on You and Your promises concerning me. In the mighty name of Jesus, Amen.

Devotional 5

Focus my eyes

"Turn my eyes away from worthless things;
preserve my life according to your word"

Psalm 119:37

I remember learning in nursing school, how the assessment should be conducted to provide a complete picture of a person whereby, the instructor could visualize the patient without ever laying eyes on them. We also learned the necessity of at times completing a focused assessment. The focused assessment was more direct and centered on a particular body system or issue. When faced with a difficult day at work or in your personal life it is easy to become overwhelmed and wish to throw in the towel. However, on those days you must focus. Focus your eyes on the solution, and not the problem. Take a deep breath, roll up your sleeves and find your inner strength to get through it. The word of God has already declared you victorious, believe even when you cannot see it!

Prayer: Father, in the name of Jesus, even when my eyes cannot see it, I will trust the promises found in Your word concerning my life. Help me to focus my eyes on You, in the mighty name of Jesus, Amen.

Devotional 6

It is me, Oh Lord

"Why do you look at the speck that is in your brother's eye, but do not notice the log that is in your own eye?"

Matthew 7:3

I remember working as a new graduate many, many years ago and becoming frustrated with my mentor on one particular day. I had just started making the transition to taking my own patient assignment, and I was becoming overwhelmed. I was upset with her and thought she was lazy as she did not immediately step in. Meanwhile, she was observing me and working behind the scenes to help me. We ended up having a conversation, and I discovered my judgment of her was wrong as she was helping me all along. In times when we feel the need to judge others in work or our personal life, we must first begin to look within. It is easy to critique others, but what about ourselves. Let your greatest work today be to critique yourself more than others.

Prayer: Father, in the name of Jesus, help me to critique myself and live a life pleasing to You. Help me to see with Christ-like eyes and esteem others more highly than myself, in the mighty name of Jesus, Amen.

Chapter 3

~THE EARS~

The Ears

The ears provide another example of God's splendor on the earth. One of the most wonderful sounds is the sound of a baby calling Ma-Ma or Da-Da for the first time. How often do you take a moment to simply thank God for your ears and the ability to hear? We do not think on this often, as we take our ability to hear for granted. Think about how challenging it would be to live in a world without being able to listen to the many beautiful sounds we have grown accustomed to hearing. Imagine missing the sound of birds singing, beautiful music, and the voices of those we hold so near. The voice of God is soothing, quiet and still. He often speaks to us in prayer and through studying His word. Take time to be intentional each day to tune your ears to hear His instruction. How precious is the one who takes the time to listen to the voice of God!

Devotional 7

Listen for wisdom

*"Turning your ear to wisdom
and applying your heart to understanding."*

Proverbs 2:2

My mother was one of the wisest people I've ever known. She shared pearls of wisdom on a daily basis. The voice of wisdom tends to somehow resonate within your soul. It's like the words have a perfect fit for your situation. Tune in your ears to wisdom, and begin to hear the voice of God for your every situation. The book of wisdom is found in the biblical proverbs. Take time this week to read the biblical proverbs and enhance your wisdom.

Prayer: Father, in the name of Jesus, thank You for words which are always wise. Help me to listen for the voice of wisdom in my life and career, in the mighty name of Jesus, Amen.

Devotional 8

God hears you

"Before they call I will answer;
while they are still speaking, I will hear".

Isaiah 65:24

I remember when my sons were younger; they would attempt to stay outside and play later than the agreed upon time. I would have to call for them, and much like myself, I would hear other parents calling for their children. However, my children could always recognize my voice and knew without a doubt the meaning of my tone. It is incredible that we have the privilege of knowing when we call on God, He hears us, and is waiting to give an answer. He has provided the answer even before we call. Likewise, in a world filled with many voices, the voice of God is sure and strong. The more time you spend training your ears to hear Him, the clearer His voice becomes.

Prayer: Father, in the name of Jesus, please incline Your ears to my voice. Lord, hear my prayers and continually allow me into Your most holy presence, in the mighty name of Jesus, Amen

Devotional 9

Ears to hear

"Ears that hear and eyes that see—
the LORD has made them both."

Proverbs 20:12

Have you ever engaged in conversation with a pessimist? I can remember once working with a very pessimistic colleague. Even when the census load was good, and we had plenty of help, she managed to have a bleak outlook continually. I noticed on days when I worked with her, even when I elected to refrain from commenting, my outlook also became pessimistic. I was not talking, yet I was listening. Listening to negativity does have an impact on your outlook. God gave us ears to hear, yet we must learn to filter out the negative voices. Make a decision to tune in to the voice of the Lord, silence inner doubt, and filter out negativity. You will then be amazed at how quickly your outlook changes!

Prayer: Father in the name of Jesus, in a world where negative words are many, allow my positive mind and positive thoughts to filter out the noise. Help me to approach each and every situation with a positive outlook, in the name of Jesus, Amen.

Chapter 4

~THE HEART~

The Heart

The heart, in my opinion, is the most powerful muscle in the body. I find it absolutely amazing how this small muscle manages to pump blood throughout the entire body. I worked early on in my nursing career with telemetry patients. I remember being so afraid anytime a monitor would beep. I would initially race to the room expecting the worst until I learned to decipher the different beeps and bleeps of the machine. Some of the beeps indicated a serious change in the patient's condition, whilst others were simply present when the patient was active. How can we learn to recognize the condition of our own heart? There is only one who knows the condition of the heart, and He is the creator of all. Search my heart, Oh Lord, and make it new!

Devotional 10

A humble heart

"Take my yoke upon you and learn from me, for I am gentle and humble in heart, and you will find rest for your souls."

Matthew 11:29

Growing up, I had a childhood friend whom I shared all of my innermost thoughts and feelings with. Over the years due to life and work, we do not have the opportunity to talk as often as we did during our childhood. However, even now when we do get the chance to chat, we simply pick up where we left off, like nothing changed between us. God is more than a lifelong friend; he longs to hear from us on a daily basis and in a more intimate way. The more time you spend with Him, you will learn the heart of God. Just like a trusted old friend, your heart is safe with him; he is your resting place.

Prayer: Father, in the name of Jesus, help me to place my yoke in your hands. Help me to learn your heart, and gentle ways, in the mighty name of Jesus, Amen.

Devotional 11

A pure heart

"Create in me a pure heart, O God,
and renew a steadfast spirit within me."

Psalm 51:10

We live in a fast-paced, technological society. Through the use of angles, and filters an individual can transform their entire appearance within minutes. Angles and filters are used with such ease, and many cannot imagine taking a picture without them. Somehow, these minor alterations have become a way of life, and a way to improve or change the look in a picture. It is important to remember though you can alter the outside, the inside is an accurate reflection of your individual identity. There is no an angle or filter to mask a contaminated heart. No one can know the heart except the one who created every one of us. Don't allow the Devil to contaminate your heart with negativity, anger, malice, pride or wicked things in the sight of God. Take time to ask the Holy Spirit to examine your heart, without a filter and to make new any area that is contrary to the work or actions of God.

Prayer: Father, in the name of Jesus, create within me a pure heart each and every day. Refresh me Oh God, with thy tender and loving spirit, in the mighty name of Jesus, Amen.

Devotional 12

A guarded heart

"Above all else, guard your heart,
for everything you do flows from it."

Proverbs 4:23

I can remember working for a period of time on a busy, medical-surgical unit where we would have prisoners assigned. The prisoners, of course, would have a guard sitting in the room who was responsible for keeping a watchful eye. The guard kept watch to be sure the prisoner did not leave, but also made sure that only authorized personnel were allowed to enter into the room. Guarding your heart is a daily, intentional effort. Setting a guard around your heart includes daily communing with our savior, and ridding ourselves of negative thinking and actions. Every single action we take flows from the heart. Each day, we must confess our flaws to God. We must be truthful with God in order for our heart to remain pure. Honesty with God and a pure heart will allow us to enter into the joy and rest of the Lord.

Prayer: Father, in the name of Jesus, help me to keep a guard upon my heart. Each day, as I enter into your presence purify my heart and mind. Help me rid myself of any negativity that would hinder your plans for my life, in the mighty name of Jesus, Amen.

Chapter 5

~THE MOUTH~

The Mouth

The mouth is a very powerful weapon. The mouth provides several functions. As nurses, we are tasked with educating patients, families, and communities on proper nutrition and the importance of watching what we put into our mouth. The evidence of how well we watch what we place in our mouth is visible with weight gain, and sicknesses to include hypertension, diabetes and many more. However, we do not take the same diligence with watching what comes out of our mouth. The words of our mouth are interconnected to our heart. Sadly, many of us speak more than we listen. It is for this reason that we must learn to think before we speak. Our words have power. Imagine for a second if every, single word you spoke instantly happened. Would you then be more diligent regarding what comes out of your mouth? Spend time studying the word of God, entering into his presence through prayer, and watch him transform your words. He will teach you on how and when to speak, and how and when not to.

Devotional 13

An answer for everyone

"Let your conversation be always full of grace, seasoned with salt, so that you may know how to answer everyone."

Colossians 4:6

Have you ever been asked a really difficult question? How about taking a test and coming to a question and not having a clue about the answer? I remember my first nursing school test. Some of the answers I knew right away, whilst others I had to think a little deeper. My frame of reference was from the words I had studied in my textbook prior to the test. Studying the word of God daily is a great way for you to stitch His words upon your heart. Then, when you are faced with a difficult question you will have an answer for every situation through the word of God.

Prayer: Father, in the name of Jesus help me to learn the power of Your word. Give me new insight into Your word each day. Create in me a passion for studying Your word and for seeking Your presence each day, in the mighty name of Jesus, Amen.

Devotional 14

Taming the tongue

"but no human being can tame the tongue. It is a restless evil, full of deadly poison."

James 3:8

Don't allow the Devil to tempt you into speaking evil or cursed words into your life. Command each and every day with the fruit of your lips. Start your morning off on the right foot by beginning with adoration and praise unto the Lord. Ask the Lord to help you throughout the day to guard the words that come from your mouth. Commit to reading His word and confess with your mouth His promises as you face each day.

Meditate on His word throughout the day and be filled with the knowledge of God's word. When tempted to speak negatively, instead declare, "God is with me today, and together we can handle whatever we may face."

Prayer: Father, in the name of Jesus, allow me to think before I speak.

Help me Lord to speak your blessings and promises over my life each day. Lord, when I am faced with challenges help me to recall the power of my words, in the mighty name of Jesus, Amen.

Devotional 15

Praise the Lord

"Open my lips, Lord,
and my mouth will declare your praise."

Psalm 51: 15

Taking time to praise the Lord each morning sets the pace for your entire day. Make it a daily habit to thank God as soon as you open your eyes. Start your day with worship, open your lips with praise. As you start to speak words of thanksgiving unto God, he will give you much more to be thankful for. Truly the Lord is excellent, wonderful are his ways!

Prayer: Father, in the name of Jesus, I am so thankful to you. I will sing praises to you all the day long. Help to thank you for every blessing great and small, in the mighty name of Jesus, Amen.

Chapter 6

~THE HANDS~

The Hands

One of the essential functions of a nurse is to touch lives. The hands
serve as a tool to assist us in the provision of care. We use our hands to
carry out our daily duties, but most importantly we use our hands to
provide a comforting touch. A comforting touch to someone in need, is
like a sip of water in a desert land. A simple touch can make all the
world of difference to someone in need. We should be ever mindful of
the power in our hands and remember each day to thank the Master for
our hands.

Devotional 16

Lift up your hands

*"Lift up your hands in the sanctuary
and praise the* LORD.*"*

Psalm 134:2

Praise is reflected with hands lifted unto the Lord. Praise is one way to become strengthened and renewed each day. Though we love our calling, nursing can be draining physically, emotionally, and mentally. Taking the time to be strengthened through praise each day is one method to achieve strength for whatever you may face in your oncoming shift. God does not intend for us to walk alone. He is willing and available to walk and talk with you throughout the day. Surrender to him, lift your hands in adoration, and give him thanks!

Prayer: Father, in the name of Jesus, when my strength begins to fail, help me to posture my heart in praise. I will lift my hands in praise, and bless Your holy name, in the mighty name of Jesus, Amen.

Devotion 17

His hands

"The heavens declare the glory of God;
the skies proclaim the work of his hands."

Psalm 19:1

I remember growing up and attending vacation bible school during the summer. One of my most cherished memories is when we learned to sing, "He's got the whole world in His hands, he's got the whole world in His hands, he's got the whole world in His hands, he's got the whole world in His hands"! Even as an adult those simple lyrics are a reminder of the power of His hands. God truly does have the whole world in His hands. When we are faced with challenges, it is easy to want to throw in the towel. Remember during those times, He has you in His hands and He will take care of you. Take notice of the above passage of scripture it begins with declaring His glory, and then the work of His hands. When you are faced with a challenge, declare the splendor of His glory, and then wait for His hands to move on your behalf.

Prayer: Father, in the name of Jesus, thank you for Your hands in my life. I am grateful to You for every blessing in my life. Teach me to trust You even when I cannot trace You, in the mighty name of Jesus, Amen.

Devotional 18

Just one touch

"She said to herself, "If I only touch his cloak, I will be healed."

Matthew 9:21

I worked for a long period of time in the home health setting. I remember on one particular occasion, I was experiencing a few personal challenges. I had developed a bond with my patients and eagerly looked forward to our visits. Anyhow, on this particular day, my words were few, and my smile must have been different than on other days. One of my patients took notice and just simply grabbed my hands. She did not say a word, nor did I, her presence in that moment, was exactly what I needed. Touch is powerful, may we never forget, how just one touch may make the difference in our patients' lives.

Prayer: Father, in the name of Jesus, touch me today and every day. Help me to touch others and be your hands here on the earth; I love you, Lord, in the mighty name of Jesus, Amen.

Chapter 7

~THE FEET~

The Feet

_____

In our culture, the feet are considered as one of the dirtiest parts of the body. But, we should not take for granted the important role that our feet play in our lives. The feet are an extension of our legs, and they help us to move and perform our daily functions. As nurses, we are well aware of the important role of our feet in the provision of patient care. Have you ever worn a pair of improperly fitting shoes on duty? I have, and by the end of my shift, I was ready to throw them in the garbage and walk barefoot. It is noticeable also, that when our feet hurt, it makes everything else seem to be out of sorts. You don't think right when your feet are hurting, and it makes your fuse just a little shorter with others. Life would be very challenging if we did not have feet. We need the Lord to guide our footsteps continually. Lord, I thank you for my feet!

Devotional 19

A lamp unto my feet

*"Your word is a lamp for my feet,
a light on my path."*

Psalm 119:105

During hurricane season, an ever-present concern is the loss of power. In times when we do not have power, we are enclosed with darkness and have limited visibility. A lamp must be plugged into an electrical socket with power in order to illuminate the darkness. In order for our path to be straight, we must plug into God. We can plug into the Lord by seeking him in prayer, reading His word daily, and communing with him for direction. Stay plugged into God, and watch him set a light for you!

Prayer: Father, in the name of Jesus, you are a lamp unto my feet and the light for my path. Help me to trust you in guiding me on which paths to take, in the mighty name of Jesus, Amen.

Devotional 20

Washing others feet

"After that, he poured water into a basin and began to wash his disciples' feet, drying them with the towel that was wrapped around him."

John 13:5

As nurses, our very profession is hinged upon serving and humility. Jesus, the savior of the world, served others through the washing of their feet. The call to serve others is evidence of Christian values at work in our career and personal lives. During my time as a home health nurse, I recollect visiting a sweet, little lady who was experiencing a number of health challenges. She was wheelchair-bound and unable to properly clean her home. She was embarrassed by the condition of her home and would try to make things presentable for my visits. On one occasion, she began to shed tears about how she wished she could clean up and walk around like in times past. Apparently, she had spent her entire life serving others and was down on life because of her present situation. I talked to her and explained how God sometimes sits us down so he can reward us, and allow others to serve us. The greatest joy comes from giving and serving others. Take a moment and give praise to our God for allowing you to be in a wonderful, helping profession where we serve others as the hands and feet of Jesus in the earth!

Prayer: Father, in the name of Jesus, I am grateful to you for my calling to serve. Help me to seek new ways and place in my path someone I can serve, in the mighty name of Jesus, Amen.

Devotional 21

Paths for your feet

*"Give careful thought to the paths for your feet
and be steadfast in all your ways."*

Proverbs 4:26

One of the most rewarding aspects of being a nurse is the ability to transition into new areas or specialties when one becomes frustrated in the present role. I remember experiencing burn-out during my career, and briefly contemplated leaving nursing all together. I am glad for guidance from the Lord, which led me to try something new. Take time to hear what God has to say to you regarding your life. He will make plain the path for your life and guide your feet. He truly does care about every area of your life, including your career. Prepare your ears to hear him, listen to his voice, God is eager to reveal his plan to you.

Prayer: Father, in the name of Jesus, thank you for creating paths for my feet. I surrender all of my thoughts and plans to you. Help me to hear your voice, and follow your directions, in the mighty name of Jesus, Amen.

Chapter 8

PRAYERS

Salvation Prayer

Father God, I have tried it my way and failed. I know that I am a sinner in need of salvation. No longer will I do it my way, I ask You to take the lead and guide me throughout my life. In faith, I accept the gift of salvation made possible through the precious blood of Jesus on the cross. I now accept You as Lord and Savior of my life. Thank You father for sending Jesus. I believe that You, Jesus are the son of God who died on the cross for my sins and rose from the dead on the third day. Thank You for bearing my sins, and the cross that I could not bear. Thank You for the gift of eternal life. I believe Your words are true, and I accept You as the power source in my life. Come into my heart, Lord Jesus and be my savior.

Amen

Prayer for Encouragement

Heavenly father, thank You for taking the lead in my life. Thank You for being here when I am lost, discouraged and afraid. Help me to be renewed in heart, and mind each and every day. Encourage my heart through Your word. Lord, grant me strength to make it through this day. I will forever sing your praises, in Jesus mighty name,

Amen

Prayer for Nurses

Father God, in the name of Jesus, You are the source of my strength and I thank You for my divine calling to serve others. Equip me to serve each day with the humility of Christ. Help me to comfort all who are in need, and give me wisdom with my words. When I am unsure of my direction, help me to seek Your wisdom, and find comfort in You. Open my heart to the needs of others and help me to provide compassionate care when it is needed most. Let me display Your love and serve as Your hands and feet here on earth, in the mighty name of Jesus, Amen.

7 Keys to building your Relationship with the Holy Spirit

1. **Become aware:** make yourself aware, He lives on the inside of you and He longs to commune with you daily. **"And I will ask the Father, and He will give you another advocate to help you and be with you forever— the Spirit of truth. The world cannot accept Him, because it neither sees Him nor knows Him. _But you know Him, for He lives with You and will be in You._(John 14:16-17)**

2. **Believe:** believing is very important. Unbelief hinders the very possibility of your prayers and relationship with him. And without faith it is impossible to please God, because _**anyone who comes to Him must believe that He exists and that He rewards those who earnestly seek Him**_**. (Hebrews 11:6).**

3. **Worship:** worship is the key that unlocks the door into His presence. Take time to worship Him not for what He has or can do for you, but simply because of who He is. Enter His gates with thanksgiving and His courts with praise; _**give thanks to Him and praise His name.**_ **(Psalm 100:4)**

4. **Prayer:** prayer is an important component of daily fellowship. Pray and speak His promises and will for your

life. His promises and will are found in the word of God. This is the confidence we have in approaching God: that *if we ask anything according to his will, He hears us.*(1 **John 5:14**)

5. **Spend time with Him:** take the initiative to carve out time daily to get to know him. Learn His voice and pursue Him **(He is a person, not an IT or THING!!)** When the Advocate comes, whom I will send to you from the Father —the Spirit of truth who goes out from the Father—*He will testify about me.* **(John 15:26)**

6. **Have no other God before him**: He is the only one who can fill all of Your voids. He is the answer to everything you have ever desired or longed for. The fullness of joy is found with Him. Jesus replied: *"Love the Lord your God with all your heart and with all your soul and with all your mind.***(Matthew 22:37)**

7. **Avoid behaviors that grieve Him:** grieving Him extends beyond the obvious fleshly sins that we ordinarily think on. Grieving Him can occur when we do not love right, when we walk in unforgiveness, when we gossip, and when we choose to live our lives in an unholy manner. We must make the choice daily to embrace His love, seek forgiveness, and be cleansed continuously in the precious blood of Jesus. And *do not grieve the Holy Spirit of God,* with whom you were sealed for the day of redemption. **(Ephesians 4:30)**

Scriptures to Renew Hope

- But those **who hope in the Lord will renew their strength**. They will soar on wings like eagles; they will run and not grow weary, they will walk and not be faint. **(Isaiah 40:31)**
- And the God of all grace, who called you to his eternal glory in Christ, after you have suffered a little while, will **himself restore you and make you strong, firm and steadfast.**(I Peter 5:10)
- And **hope does not put us to shame**, because God's love has been poured out into our hearts through the Holy Spirit, who has been given to us. **(Romans 5:5)**
- May the **God of hope** fill you with all joy and peace as you trust in Him, so that you may **overflow with hope by the power of the Holy Spirit.** (Romans 15:13)
- Oh, that **I might have my request**, God would grant **what I hope for**. (Job 6:8)
- Be strong and take heart, all you **who hope in the Lord.** (Psalm 31:24)
- Trust **in the Lord with all your heart** and lean not on your

own understanding in all your ways submit to Him, and **he will make your paths straight**. (Proverbs 3:5-6)

- **Peace I leave with you; my peace I give you**. I do not give to you as the world gives. **Do not let your hearts be troubled and do not be afraid**. (John 14:27)
- For the Spirit God gave us does not make us timid, **but gives us power, love and self-discipline. (2 Timothy 1:7)**

Affirmations for Nurses

- **I am blessed and highly favored!** The favor and blessings of God are upon me.
- **I am focused and ready to slay today!** Today, my mind is focused and I can handle whatever this day brings through Christ (Philippians 4:13).
- **I am striving each day to be the best nurse I can be!** I am created to serve and I will provide excellent nursing care.
- **I am filled with the joy and peace of the Lord!** God is my peace and he brings the fullness of joy into my life.
- **I am healthy and my mind is brilliant!** God strengths my body and mind each day.

Made in the USA
Columbia, SC
07 December 2023

28022541R00052